Filipino
homestyle dishes

One of Asia's least known but most exciting cuisines
features delicious dishes such as Spicy Garlic Shrimp
(Gambas) and Braised Pork with Vegetables (Pinakbet).

Norma Olizon-Chikiamco

PERIPLUS

Contents

MAIL ORDER SOURCES

Finding the ingredients for Asian home cooking has become very simple. Most supermarkets carry staples such as soy sauce, fresh ginger and fresh lemongrass. Almost every large metropolitan area has Asian markets serving the local population—just check your local business directory. With the Internet, exotic Asian ingredients and cooking utensils can be easily found online. The following list is a good starting point of online merchants offering a wide variety of goods and services.

http://www.asiafoods.com

http://www.geocities.com/MadisonAvenue/8074/VarorE.html

http://dmoz.org/Shopping/Food/Ethnic_and_Regional/Asian/

http://templeofthai.com/

http://www.orientalpantry.com/

http://www.zestyfoods.com/

http://www.thaigrocer.com/Merchant/index.htm

http://asianwok.com/

http://pilipinomart.com/

http://www.ramarfoods.com/main.asp?p=home

Filipino food is one of the least well-known of all Southeast Asian cuisines. Strongly influenced by the historical presence of the Spaniards, Chinese and Americans, it lacks the singular national identity that characterizes the food of other nations. Any mention of Filipino food would probably draw a blank from most people who can't associate it with any dish in particular. What is it? How does it taste? How does one cook it?

Yet it is precisely this indefinable quality, this veil of mystery surrounding it, that makes Filipino food an interesting discovery.

Imagine a stew of slowly tenderized beef, its sauce thickened by long, patient simmering, enriched with the flavors of olive oil and grated cheese. Or a pot of backyard vegetables cooked in shrimp paste and a spell of garlic, garnished with morsels of cubed pork. Or a parfait of tropical fruits and beans, sweetened with sugar and milk and topped with crushed ice. These, and more, are all part of the repertoire of the Filipino cook. They show the diversity of Filipino cuisine—from the Spanish-influenced Caldereta, to the indigenous Pinakbet, to the Asian-inspired Halo-halo mélange.

This diversity is likewise reflected in the wide variety of ingredients used in Filipino cooking. While some dishes may call for the liberal application of Spanish olive oil, others are more Oriental in their use of Asian condiments such as soy sauce and shrimp paste. Moreover, not only are these condiments used during the cooking process; often they are also served at the table as dips, so that diners can customize the flavor of the dishes according to their own tastes.

Many Filipino dishes are also characterized by heavy sauces. While this may seem strange to some, to Filipinos it makes perfect sense. The sauces in a dish are often used to soften and flavor the rice with which the dish is eaten. Thus, dishes such as Stewed Pork (Estofado) are seldom served dry. These sauces are to Filipinos what gravy is to the Americans or Europeans.

With the advent of globalization, many Filipinos are now more aware of the cuisines of other countries. Modern appliances have also made cooking a much easier task than it was a century ago. Yet while hamburgers and pasta may sometimes be cooked in the contemporary Filipino kitchen, more often it is the standard Filipino dishes that rule. There will always be Adobo, Menudo and fish sauce, shrimp paste and soy sauce in a Filipino kitchen, whether it be in the urban climes of Manila or in the rugged terrain of Abra.

This collection of recipes presents authentic Filipino dishes as they would be cooked in a Filipino home. Many are personal favorites in my own family; all have been kitchen tested and are representative of true Filipino cuisine, in all its diversity, simplicity and complexity. They are a magical discovery of the food of a resilient people who, while adopting foreign influences, have managed to create a cuisine that is truly their own—part Western, part Oriental, and uniquely, enchantingly Filipino.

Basic Filipino Ingredients

Almond essence or almond extract is sold in small bottles in the baking section of supermarkets. If almond essence is not available, substitute with vanilla extract.

Annatto seeds, known as *atsuete* in the Philippines, are dried, reddish-brown seeds that are used as a food coloring or dye. The seeds are soaked, then squeezed in water to extract the red coloring, which lends an orange to reddish tint to food. Artificial red food coloring may be substituted.

Banana heart is the tender innermost portion of the stem of the young banana plant. It is cooked as a vegetable and is available fresh in Asian grocery stores.

Bitter gourds, known in the Philippines as *ampalaya*, are green and resemble fluted cucumbers. They are available fresh from Asian grocery stores. Bitter gourds are sometimes salted before cooking to eliminate their bitter taste. If bitter gourd is unavailable, substitute winter melon or cucumber.

Chayote, known as *sayote* in the Philippines, or christophene or choko, is a pale green squash that resembles a wrinkled pear. It should be peeled before use. If chayote is not available, substitute zucchini.

Chicharon or deep-fried pork cracklings, are thin pieces of pork rind that are grilled and then deep-fried until crispy. They are sold in packets and are available in Asian grocery stores.

Chilies come in two basic varieties; the small (about 1 in/2$^{1}/_{2}$ cm in length) and very hot chilies are known as *siling labuyo* in the Philippines, or *chili padi* in Malaysia and Singapore (and are commonly referred to as "bird's eye chilies" elsewhere). These are often chopped and used in dipping sauces. *Siling labuyo* chilies are used sparingly —the amount of heat increases as the size diminishes. The longer finger-length chilies, known as *siling mahaba* in Tagalog, are often cooked with soups and stir-fries. To reduce the heat of a chili while retaining its flavor, make a lengthwise slit and remove the seeds.

Coconut cream and **coconut milk** are used in many Filipino desserts and curries. To obtain **fresh coconut cream** (which is normally used for desserts), grate the flesh of 1 coconut into a bowl (this yields about 3 cups of grated coconut flesh), add $^{1}/_{2}$ cup water and knead thoroughly a few times, then squeeze the mixture firmly in your fist or strain with a muslin cloth or cheese cloth. **Thick coconut milk** is obtained by the same method but by adding double the water to the grated flesh (about 1 cup instead of ¹/₂ cup). **Thin coconut milk** (which is used for curries rather than desserts) is obtained by pressing the grated coconut a second time— adding 1 cup of water to the same grated coconut flesh and squeezing it again. Although freshly pressed milk has more flavor, coconut cream and milk are now widely sold canned or in packets that are quick, convenient and quite tasty. Canned or packet coconut cream or milk comes in varying consistencies depending on the brand, and you will need to try them out and adjust the thickness by adding water as needed. In general, you should add 1 cup of water to 1 cup of canned or packet coconut cream to obtain thick coconut milk, or 2 cups of water to 1 cup of coconut cream to obtain thin coconut milk. These mixing ratios are only general guides however. For best results, follow the package instructions.

Coriander leaves, also known as cilantro, are widely used as a flavoring and garnish. Fresh coriander leaves have a strong taste and aroma and can be refrigerated in a plastic bag for about one week. Parsley is a suitable substitute.

Fish sauce or *patis* is made from salted, fermented fish or prawns. It is clear, golden brown in color, tastes salty, and is used in marinades, dressings and dipping sauces. It is sold in bottles and is available in Asian grocery stores and supermarkets.

Hoisin sauce is a sweet Chinese sauce made from soybeans. It is used as a dipping sauce and flavoring and is sold in jars or cans in Asian grocery stores.

Jicama, also known as yam bean or *bangkuang* in Malaysia and Singapore, is a crunchy tuber with crisp, white flesh and beige skin. It may be eaten raw with a spicy dip or may be sautéed and used as a filling in spring rolls. It is sold fresh in Asian grocery stores and supermarkets, and may be substituted with lotus root or cabbage.

Kanton **noodles** are thin noodles that are made from wheat and egg. They are available in round or flat shapes in a variety of sizes.

Palm sugar is distilled from the juice of the aren or coconut palm fruit, and has a rich flavor. Substitute with dark brown sugar, maple syrup or regular sugar with a touch of molasses.

Pan de sal is the national bread of the Philippines, usually made with salt, yeast, sugar and flour and shaped into a bun. If *pan de sal* is not available, it may be substituted with any bun or bread.

Plantains look like bananas, but are less sweet and have a firmer texture, which makes them suitable for preparation as a vegetable. They are available in Hispanic markets. If unavailable, unripe bananas or pumpkins make a reasonable substitute.

Pinipig is a rice cereal that has been flattened and

toasted in a pan to make it crunchy. It is used in desserts or as a topping. It can also be eaten as a cereal or as an accompaniment to thick hot chocolate. If *pinipig* is not available, any crispy rice cereal such as Rice Krispies may be used as a substitute.

Rice flour is sold in packets in supermarkets. It can be made in small quantities by first soaking $1/2$ cup long grain rice in water for 5 hours. Drain and transfer the rice to a blender. Add $1/2$ cup water and grind until a thick liquid mixture forms. Pour the mixture into a fine sieve and set aside until the water drains and a paste forms. Use as indicated in the recipe. This yields about $1/2$ cup rice flour.

Rice vermicelli are very fine, white threads made from rice flour. These dried noodles can be easily rehydrated by soaking in hot water for a few minutes, then rinsing before adding to soups or frying.

Sago pearls are tiny dried beads of sago obtained by grinding the pith of the sago palm to a paste and pressing it through a sieve. It is glutinous, with little taste, and is often used in Asian desserts. Sago pearls are sold in packets in Asian grocery stores. Sago pearls should not be confused with fresh sago, which is starchy and sticky.

Shrimp paste, known as *bagoong* in Tagalog, is a dried, salty paste made from fermented shrimp. It is the same as Indonesian *trasi*, Thai *kapi* or Malaysian *belachan*.

Soy sauce is brewed from wheat, salt and soy beans. Black soy sauce is dark and thick and gives a slightly smokey flavor to a dish, while regular soy sauce is thinner and saltier.

Spanish sausages, known as *chorizo*, are dried pork sausages flavored with paprika, garlic and chili. In Filipino cuisine, they are usually added to stews rather than being eaten on their own. They are available from supermarkets and may be substituted with pepperoni or any other spicy sausages.

Spring roll wrappers or *lumpia* wrappers are a thin crêpe made from a batter of rice flour, water and salt, with or without eggs. Wrappers made with eggs are known as egg roll wrappers and rolls made with this type of wrapper are normally deep-fried. Thinner rice flour wrappers come already cooked and must be moistened with a bit of water or steamed to make them flexible.

Tofu is a soy product that comes in many forms and consistencies. **Firm tofu** is sold fresh in supermarkets in sealed plastic tubs. **Pressed tofu**, known as *tokwa* in the Philippines, is tofu that has been pressed to expel most of the water.

Water spinach is a nutritious leafy green vegetable also known as water convolvulus or *kangkong*. Young shoots may be eaten raw as part of a salad platter or with a dip. The leaves and tender stems are usually braised.

Wonton wrappers are square pastry-like wrappers sold in various sizes in the refrigerator sections of supermarkets. They are filled with meats or vegetables, then fried, steamed or boiled in soups.

Lechon Sauce

$3^1/_2$ oz (100 g) chicken livers
2 tablespoons cider vinegar
$1/_4$ cup breadcrumbs
$1^1/_2$ tablespoons minced garlic
$1/_2$ cup (50 g) minced onion
$1/_2$ teaspoon salt, adding extra to taste
$1/_4$ teaspoon pepper, adding extra to taste
1 tablespoon dark brown sugar or palm sugar
$1/_2$ cup (125 ml) water

1 Grill the chicken livers under a broiler until half cooked, about 3–4 minutes, then press the livers through a sieve to extract the juices and soft meat. Discard the remaining parts of the livers.
2 Combine the chicken liver juices with the remaining ingredients in a saucepan and simmer over medium heat until mixture thickens, about 30 minutes.
3 Serve with Deep-fried Pork (see page 69).

Makes about 1 cup
Preparation time: **10 mins**
Cooking time: **30 mins**

Garlic Vinegar Dip

$1/_2$ cup (125 ml) vinegar
4–5 cloves garlic, peeled and crushed
$1/_4$ teaspoon freshly ground black pepper, adding extra to taste

1 Combine the vinegar, garlic and black pepper in a bowl then set aside.
2 Serve with Deep-fried Pork (page 69) or Filipino Sausages (page 73)

Makes about $1/_2$ cup
Preparation time: **5 mins**

Sour Cream-Mayonnaise Dip

$1/_2$ cup mayonnaise
$1/_2$ cup sour cream
3–4 cloves garlic, minced
1 teaspoon *adobo* seasoning (optional)
1 teaspoon salt
$1/_2$ teaspoon pepper

1 In a bowl, mix mayonnaise and sour cream to form a smooth mixture. Add garlic and adobo seasoning, if desired. Season with salt and pepper to taste.
2 Serve as a dip with deep-fried dishes.

Makes about 1 cup
Preparation time: **5 mins**

Grilled Eggplant Relish

8 oz (225 g) eggplants
1 tablespoon lime juice
2–3 cloves garlic, crushed
2 tablespoons vinegar
$1/2$ teaspoon salt
$1/4$ teaspoon pepper
1 small tomato, diced
1 scallion, chopped

Makes about $1^1/_2$ cups
Preparation time:
  10–15 mins
Cooking time: **15 mins**

1 Grill the eggplants under a preheated broiler or over a barbecue grill until tender, about 15 minutes, turning frequently to cook evenly. Slice open the eggplants and scoop out the soft flesh. Finely mash the eggplant flesh with the back of a fork. Sprinkle with lime juice and set aside for a few minutes.
2 Combine the garlic and vinegar in a bowl. Pour over the mashed eggplants. Add salt and pepper. Mix well and garnish with tomato and scallions
3 Serve as relish with fried or steamed fish.

Garlic Mayonnaise Dip

$1/2$ cup (125 ml) mayon-
  naise
8–10 cloves of garlic,
  peeled and crushed
1 teaspoon white sugar
1 teaspoon Knorr or
  Maggi seasoning sauce
$1/4$ teaspoon salt, adding
  extra to taste
$1/4$ teaspoon pepper,
  adding extra to taste

1 Mix the ingredients in a bowl to form a smooth mixture.
2 Serve as a dip with Crispy Squid Rings (page 17).

If Knorr or Maggi seasoning sauce is not available, substitute with 2–3 drops of Worcestershire sauce.

Makes about $1/2$ cup
Preparation time: **5 mins**

Vinegar Lime Dip

$1/4$ cup (125 ml) soy sauce
2 tablespoons vinegar
2 tablespoons lime juice
2–3 cloves garlic, crushed
$1/2$ tablespoon sugar
1–2 scallions, chopped
2 tablespoons water
$1/4$ teaspoon pepper or
  chopped red chilies

1 Combine all the ingredients in a bowl. Set aside for several minutes to allow the flavors to blend.
2 Serve as a dip for grilled or fried fish, or grilled pork.

Makes about 1 cup
Preparation time: **5 mins**

Pickled Daikon and Carrots (Acharang Labanos)

7 oz (200 g) daikon radish, peeled and very thinly sliced, mashed with $1/2$ cup salt and set aside 3–4 hours
$3/4$ cup (150 g) sugar
$1/2$ cup (125 ml) white or cane vinegar
1 medium carrot, peeled and very thinly sliced

Makes 2 cups
Preparation time: **20 mins + 3–4 hours soaking**
Cooking time: **10 mins**

1 Rinse salted radishes in water thoroughly, making sure to remove all the salt. Press out all the water and set aside.

2 Combine sugar and vinegar in a saucepan and stir. Simmer over low heat until mixture becomes clear, about 3 minutes. Add the radish and carrots. Simmer for about 5 minutes.

3 Remove from heat and, using a slotted spoon, transfer radish and carrots to a clean glass bowl. Pour in a little of the vinegar-sugar syrup. Set aside to cool. Store in a covered container. Refrigerate and serve with fried fish, fried chicken or grilled dishes.

Green Mango and Tomato Relish

1 green unripe mango (about 5 oz/150 g)
2–3 small ripe tomatoes, diced
1 small onion, minced
1 tablespoon sugar, adding extra to taste
2 tablespoons fish sauce
1 tablespoon lime juice

Serves 4
Preparation time: **10 mins**

1 Peel and dice the mango, discarding the mango seed. Combine the mango with the tomatoes and onions.

2 Mix the sugar, fish sauce and lime juice. Pour over the mango mixture and stir. Set aside for 5–10 minutes before serving.

3 Serve with Cured Pork (page 68), Chicken and Pork Adobo (page 62) or fried fish dishes.

Cut wrapper into two. Spoon 2 tablespoons of ground pork mixture onto each wrapper.

Moisten edges of wrapper with egg and water mixture. Roll wrapper and seal the edges.

Tasty Pork and Shrimp Spring Rolls
(Lumpiang Shanghai)

2 tablespoons oil
2 tablespoons finely
  minced garlic
$1/2$ cup diced onions
1 lb (450 g) ground pork
6 oz (180 g) fresh shrimp,
  peeled, deveined and
  diced
$1/4$ cup chopped scallions
$1/2$ cup julienned jicama
1 medium carrot, grated
$1/4$ teaspoon salt, adding
  extra to taste
$1/4$ teaspoon pepper,
  adding extra to taste
1 egg
1–2 tablespoons water
20 spring roll wrappers
3 cups (750 ml) oil for
  deep-frying

Sweet and Sour Sauce
$1/4$ cup (50 g) sugar
$1/4$ teaspoon salt
2 tablespoons tomato
  ketchup
$1/4$ cup (60 ml) vinegar
1 tablespoon cornstarch
  dissolved in $1/2$ cup
  (125 ml) water

1 To make the Sweet and Sour Sauce, blend the sugar, salt, tomato ketchup and vinegar in a saucepan. Simmer over low heat. Stir in the cornstarch mixture. Continue simmering, stirring occasionally, until the sauce thickens. Turn off heat and set aside.

2 Heat the oil in a frying pan and sauté the garlic and onions. Add pork and and sauté until lightly browned. Add the shrimp, scallions, jicama and carrot and sauté until pork is cooked through, stirring to mix well. Season with the salt and pepper. Set aside to cool.

3 Combine egg and water in a small bowl. Cut each spring roll wrapper in half. Spoon about 2 tablespoons of the ground pork and shrimp mixture onto each wrapper. Moisten the edges of each wrapper with the egg mixture. Roll each wrapper, folding in the ends, then seal the edges.

4 Heat half of the oil in a frying pan over high heat until hot, then reduce the heat. Fry the rolls in batches in the hot oil until browned, adding more oil as needed. Serve hot with the Sweet and Sour Sauce.

Makes 40 spring rolls
Preparation time: **30 mins**
Cooking time: **40 mins**

Papaya Relish (Papaya Achara)

1 small unripe papaya,
(about 10 oz/300 g)
2 teaspoons salt
$^3/_4$ cup (150 g) sugar
$^3/_4$ cup (185 ml) white
vinegar
$^1/_2$ teaspoon salt
1 small carrot, thinly sliced
$^1/_2$ red bell pepper, thinly
sliced
$^1/_2$ green bell pepper,
thinly sliced
8–10 thin slices ginger
$^1/_4$ cup (25 g) raisins

Syrup
$^3/_4$ cup (150 g) sugar
$^1/_2$ cup (125 ml) cane or
white vinegar
$^1/_2$ teaspoon salt

1 Peel the papaya then grate into thin strips. Coat the papaya strips well with 2 teaspoons of salt. Rinse and squeeze out any juice. Pat dry with paper towels.
2 Mix the sugar, vinegar and $^1/_2$ teaspoon of salt in a large saucepan. Add the papaya strips and simmer for about 5 minutes. Add carrots and bell peppers and simmer for 5 minutes, or until carrots are tender. Drain and arrange in a bowl.
3 Soak the ginger slices in hot water and drain. Toss ginger and raisins with the cooked vegetables.
4 Combine the Syrup ingredients in a separate saucepan. Bring to a boil, lower heat and simmer for 5 minutes. Pour the Syrup over the cooked vegetables.
5 Set aside to cool then transfer to a container and cover. If not using immediately, store in a refrigerator. Serve with roasted or fried meats.

Serves 4–6
Preparation time: **30 mins**
Cooking time: **20 mins**

Green Salad (Ensaladang Pinoy)

5–6 large lettuce leaves, torn
2 medium tomatoes, quartered
1 small cucumber, thinly sliced
$1/2$ medium yellow onion, thinly sliced

Dressing
$1/2$ cup (100 g) superfine sugar
$3/4$ cup (185 ml) vinegar
$1/2$ teaspoon salt
$1/2$ tablespoon fish sauce
$1/4$ teaspoon freshly ground black pepper

1 To make the Dressing, combine the sugar, vinegar, salt and fish sauce in a bowl and stir well. Add the ground black pepper then set aside for a few minutes.
2 Toss the lettuce leaves, tomatoes, cucumber and onions.
3 Pour the Dressing over the tossed vegetables just before serving.

Serves 4–6
Preparation time: **15 mins**

Spicy Garlic Shrimp (Gambas)

1 lb (450 g) fresh medium shrimp, peeled and deveined
1 tablespoon lime juice
2 tablespoons oil
3 tablespoons crushed garlic
$1/4$ teaspoon Tabasco or other hot pepper sauce
$1/4$ teaspoon salt, adding extra to taste
$1/4$ teaspoon freshly ground black pepper, adding extra to taste
Few sprigs parsley, to garnish (optional)
1 green chili, thinly sliced, to garnish (optional)

1 Marinate the peeled shrimp in the lime juice for about 30 minutes.

2 Heat the oil in a frying pan or wok and sauté garlic until lightly browned. Add shrimp and stir-fry until they turn pink, about 3 minutes.

3 Season with hot pepper sauce and salt and pepper to taste. Transfer to a serving dish and garnish with parsley and sliced chilies if desired.

Serves 4–6
Preparation time: **20 mins + 30 mins marinating**
Cooking time: **5 mins**

Braised Vegetables with Fish (Dinengdeng)

$^1/_4$ cup (60 ml) oil

2–4 small fish or 1 lb (450 g) fish fillets (any fish may be used, such as mackerel, scad or tilapia)

1 lb (450 g) chayote or squash, peeled and cut into bite-sized pieces

10 oz (300 g) eggplant, cut into bite-sized pieces

$3^1/_2$ oz (100 g) green beans, sliced into 2-in (5-cm) pieces

2 tablespoons shrimp paste

$^1/_4$ cup (60 ml) water

1 Heat the oil in a frying pan and fry the fish for 2–3 minutes on each side, or until golden brown. Set aside to cool slightly, then slice. Place the chayote, eggplants, green beans and fish slices in a large saucepan.

2 Mix the shrimp paste with water until smooth, then pour into the saucepan.

3 Simmer over medium heat for 10–15 minutes until vegetables are cooked but still firm.

Serves 4
Preparation time: **5 mins**
Cooking time: **25 mins**

Tofu and Pork Vinaigrette (Tokwa't Baboy)

10 oz (300 g) pork
  shoulder
8 oz (225 g) pressed tofu
  (*tokwa*)
2 tablespoons oil
1 small onion, diced
1/4 cup (60 ml) vinegar
2 tablespoons soy sauce
2 tablespoons chopped
  scallions, to garnish
  (optional)

Serves 4–6
Preparation time: **30 mins**
Cooking time: **45–50 mins**

1 Simmer the pork shoulder in water for 30 minutes or until cooked through. Drain and set aside to cool.
2 While the pork is simmering, pat the pressed tofu dry with paper towels then cut into bite-sized pieces. Heat the oil in a wok or skillet and fry the tofu pieces over medium heat in batches until they turn golden brown, 2–3 minutes each side. Remove from the heat, drain on paper towels and set aside.
3 Mix the onions, vinegar and soy sauce in a bowl. Add water to taste if the mixture is too sour. Set aside for a few minutes.
4 Slice the pork shoulder thinly and combine with the reserved tofu in a separate bowl.
5 Pour the soy sauce mixture over the pork and tofu and *stir*. Garnish with scallions, if desired, and serve with rice and other dishes.

Crispy Squid Rings (Calamares)

Often served in bars and bistros as a snack, Calamares is a dish of Spanish origin adopted by Filipinos and localized with the use of calamansi limes.

1 lb (450 g) medium squid, head, ink sacs and tentacles discarded, purple skin peeled
2 tablespoons lime juice
2 egg whites
$^1/_2$ cup (60 g) flour
1 cup (250 ml) oil
$^1/_4$ teaspoon salt, adding extra to taste
$^1/_4$ teaspoon freshly ground black pepper, adding extra to taste
Lettuce leaves, for serving (optional)

1 Slice the cleaned squid into rings. Marinate in lime juice for about 30 minutes.

2 Dip the squid rings in egg whites, then dredge in flour.

3 Heat the oil in a wok over medium heat and fry the squid rings in hot oil a few pieces at a time until they turn golden brown, about 1 minute. Do not overcook as this will make the squid tough. Remove the rings from the wok and drain on paper towels. Season with the salt and pepper.

4 Serve on a bed of lettuce leaves, with Garlic Mayonnaise Dip (see page 8) on the side, if desired.

Serves 4–6
Preparation time: **15 mins + 30 mins marinating**
Cooking time: **15–20 mins**

Vegetarian Rice Paper Rolls (Lumpiang Sariwa)

2 tablespoons oil
1 cup (200 g) pressed
   tofu (*tokwa*), diced
1 cup (100 g) green
   beans, thinly sliced on
   the diagonal
1 medium carrot, julienned
3/4 cup (100 g) thinly
   sliced white cabbage
1/4 teaspoon salt
1/4 teaspoon pepper
12 rice flour spring roll
   wrappers
Soft green or red lettuce
   leaves
1 cup (130 g) boiled
   chickpeas
Chili sauce (optional)
8–10 cloves garlic, peeled
   and crushed

Sauce
1 cup (200 g) dark brown
   sugar or palm sugar
2 cups (500 ml) water
1 teaspoon salt
2 tablespoons soy sauce
2 tablespoons cornstarch
1/4 cup (60 ml) water

1 To prepare the Sauce, blend the sugar, water, salt and soy sauce in a saucepan, bring to a boil then simmer 5 minutes. In a small bowl, mix the cornstarch and water to form a smooth mixture. Stir into the sugar-soy sauce mixture. Simmer over low heat until the mixture thickens, about 10–15 minutes.

2 Heat the oil in a pan and stir-fry the diced tofu over medium heat until browned, about 5–7 minutes. Remove from pan and set aside.

3 Blanch the green beans, carrots and cabbage in boiling water for 3–5 minutes. Drain immediately and rinse with cold water. Drain well then season with salt and pepper.

4 Steam a rice flour spring roll wrapper until soft, about 3 minutes. Line a wrapper with a small piece of lettuce leaf. Spoon 2–3 tablespoons of the blanched vegetables onto the lettuce leaf. Add 1 tablespoon of the chickpeas and the tofu. Roll the wrapper and tuck in one end to seal. Repeat with remaining ingredients. Serve with chili sauce, crushed garlic and Sauce.

Serves 4–6
Preparation time: **40 mins**
Cooking time: **30 mins**

Steam the spring roll wrappers to soften.

Line a spring roll with a lettuce leaf.

Spoon the vegetables onto the lettuce leaf.

Roll the wrapper and tuck in one end to seal.

Homestyle Chicken and Vegetable Casserole
(Nilaga)

1 chicken (2^1/$_4$ lbs/1 kg), cut into serving portions
1 onion, thinly sliced
8 cups (2 liters) water
2 potatoes, peeled and cut in chunks
2 cups thickly sliced plantains (optional)
2 tablespoons fish sauce
^{1}/$_2$ teaspoon salt
1 teaspoon pepper
1 small head cabbage, quartered

Fish Sauce Dip
^{1}/$_2$ cup (125 ml) fish sauce
2 tablespoons lime juice

1 Place chicken and onion in a large casserole and pour in the water. Bring to a boil, then lower heat to medium and simmer for 20 minutes.
2 Add the potatoes and simmer for 5 minutes. Add the plantains and simmer until the chicken, potatoes and plantains are tender, about 10 more minutes. Season with fish sauce, salt and pepper. Add the cabbage and cook until just tender, about 2 minutes.
3 To make the Fish Sauce Dip, combine the fish sauce and lime juice in a bowl.
4 Serve soup hot with rice and Fish Sauce Dip.

Serves 4–6
Preparation time: **5 mins**
Cooking time: **35–45 mins**

Healthy Papaya and Ginger Chicken Soup
(Tinola)

2 tablespoons oil
3–4 cloves garlic, minced
2 in (5 cm) ginger, peeled and thinly sliced
2 lbs (900 g) chicken pieces (breast, thighs and drumsticks)
6 cups (1 1/2 liters) water
7 oz (200 g) unripe papaya, peeled and cut into chunks
2 tablespoons fish sauce
1 tablespoon salt
1 1/2 cups (50 g) spinach or watercress leaves, washed and drained

1 Heat the oil in a large casserole and sauté garlic for 1 minute. Add ginger and chicken pieces, sauté until the chicken is lightly browned, then add the water and bring to a boil over high heat.

2 Reduce the heat to medium and simmer the chicken until almost tender, about 20 minutes. Add papaya and season with fish sauce and salt. Simmer over medium heat until the chicken is fully cooked and papaya is tender, about 10 more minutes.

3 Stir in the spinach or watercress leaves and heat through. Serve hot with additional fish sauce, if desired.

Serves 6
Preparation time: **10 mins**
Cooking time: **35 mins**

Ground Beef and Vegetable Stew (Picadillo)

2 tablespoons oil
1 onion, diced
3–4 cloves garlic, minced
1 lb (450 g) ground beef
6 cups (1 1/2 liters) beef stock (made from beef bouillon cubes) or water
2 medium potatoes, peeled and diced
2 small carrots, peeled and diced
1 cup (50 g) spinach leaves or peas
2 tablespoons fish sauce
1/2 teaspoon salt
1/2 teaspoon freshly ground black pepper

1 Heat the oil in a casserole or large saucepan and sauté the onion until transparent, 2–3 minutes. Add garlic and sauté until fragrant, about 1 minute.
2 Add the ground beef and stir-fry until browned, 3–4 minutes. Pour in the beef stock or water. Bring to a boil then simmer over medium heat. Add diced potatoes and carrots and simmer until potatoes and carrots are tender, about 10 minutes. Stir in spinach leaves or peas, and heat through. Season with fish sauce, salt and pepper and serve hot with rice.

Serves 6
Preparation time: **10 mins**
Cooking time: **20 mins**

Delicious Beef Marrow Soup (Bulalo)

3 lbs (1 1/2 kg) beef bones with marrow, sliced
1 onion, sliced
8 cups (2 liters) water
1 lb (450 g) beef shank or stewing beef, cut into chunks
2 potatoes, peeled and cut into chunks
2 cups thickly sliced plantains
1 small head cabbage, quartered
2 tablespoons fish sauce
1/4 teaspoon salt, adding extra to taste
1/4 teaspoon pepper, adding extra to taste

1 Place the sliced bones with marrow and onions in a large stockpot, pour in water and bring to a boil. Lower heat and simmer for 40 minutes. Add the beef chunks. Return to a boil, then reduce heat to medium. Simmer until beef is tender, about 1 hour.
2 Add the potatoes and plantains. Simmer until potatoes and plantains are tender, about 15 minutes. Add the cabbage. Stir in fish sauce, salt and pepper. Cook until cabbage is just tender, about 5 minutes.
3 Serve with rice and Fish Sauce Dip (see page 20).

Serves 6–8
Preparation time: **10 mins**
Cooking time: **2 1/2 hours**

Shrimp and Pork Wonton Soup (Molo Soup)

This dish is a speciality of the Visayas region of the Philippines. The secret to this dish is a tasty broth which forms the base of the soup. Preparation can be time-consuming, so allow ample time to cook and prepare it.

1 lb (450 g) ground pork
³/₄ cup (100 g) fresh or canned water chestnuts, peeled and chopped
8 oz (225 g) fresh shrimp, peeled and deveined
1 egg
2 tablespoons soy sauce
¹/₄ cup (50 g) chopped scallions
30–40 wonton wrappers
2 tablespoons oil
1 medium onion, minced
3–4 cloves garlic, minced
8 cups (2 liters) chicken stock (from chicken bones or chicken bouillon cubes)
8 oz (225 g) chicken breast fillet, sliced into thin strips
2 teaspoons fish sauce

1 Combine the ground pork and chopped water chestnuts in a mixing bowl. Chop half the shrimp coarsely and add to the bowl (set aside remaining shrimp). Mix in the egg, soy sauce and half the scallions.

2 Place wonton wrappers on a clean work surface and fill each wrapper with 1 heaped teaspoon of the pork mixture. Brush the edges of the wrappers with a little water and press edges together to seal. Set aside.

3 Heat the oil in a casserole. Sauté the onions until transparent, 2–3 minutes, then add garlic and sauté until fragrant, 1–2 minutes. Pour in the chicken stock and bring to a boil. Add the filled wonton wrappers, and reduce heat to medium.

4 Add the chicken and simmer until chicken and wontons are completely cooked, about 10–15 minutes. Stir in the reserved shrimp and simmer until shrimp turn pink, another 1–2 minutes. Season with fish sauce and garnish with remaining scallions.

Serves 8
Preparation time: **45 mins**
Cooking time: **45 mins**

Fill each wrapper with 1 heaped teaspoon of the pork mixture.

Brush the edges with water and press to seal.

Sautéed Water Spinach (Adobong Kangkong)

1 lb (450 g) water
spinach (*kangkong*)
1 tablespoon cane or
white vinegar
2 tablespoons soy sauce
$1/4$ cup (60 ml) water
1 tablespoon oyster sauce
1 tablespoon oil
4 oz (125 g) ground pork
$1/2$ medium onion, diced
3 cloves garlic, crushed

Serves 4–6
Preparation time: **5 mins**
Cooking time: **10 mins**

1 Wash and trim the water spinach, separating the
leaves from the stalks, removing and discarding the
thick lower half of the stems. Set aside.
2 Combine the vinegar, soy sauce, water and oyster
sauce in a bowl and set aside.
3 Heat the oil in a frying pan over medium heat.
Add the ground pork and sauté for 2 minutes until
browned. Push the pork to one side of the pan.
Add the onion and garlic and sauté about 1 minute.
Add the water spinach stalks and stir-fry 2 minutes,
then add the leaves. Pour in the vinegar mixture.
4 Cover the pan and simmer until the stalks and
leaves are just tender, 1–2 minutes. Do not overcook.
Serve immediately with rice.

Braised Cabbage (Guisadong Repolyo)

2 tablespoons oil
1 small onion, minced
8–10 cloves garlic,
  crushed
4 oz (125 g) ground pork
4 chicken livers, sliced
8 oz (225 g) chicken
  breast or fillet, sliced
5 cups (400 g) sliced
  cabbage
2 cups (500 ml) water
2 chicken bouillon cubes
2 tablespoons soy sauce

1 Heat the oil in a wok or casserole. Sauté the onions until transparent, 2–3 minutes. Add garlic and sauté until fragrant, about 1 minute. Add the ground pork and sauté until lightly browned. Add chicken livers and chicken breast and sauté until almost cooked. 2 Stir in the sliced cabbage. Pour in water and add the bouillon cubes. Simmer over medium heat until cabbage is just tender, about 3 minutes. Season with soy sauce.

Serves 6
Preparation time: **15 mins**
Cooking time: **15–20 mins**

Braised Pork with Vegetables (Pinakbet)

A favorite dish in the Ilocos region, this has also become popular in other parts of the Philippines. The trick to cooking Pinakbet is not to stir the vegetables during the cooking process as this could make the dish bitter. Pungent dried shrimp paste is the main flavoring for this dish.

1–2 tablespoons coarse salt
1 bitter gourd, (about 5 oz/150 g), seeded and sliced into small pieces
$1/2$ cup (125 ml) cane or white vinegar
8 oz (225 g) pork belly or pork loin, sliced
1 cup (250 ml) water
2 tablespoons oil
1 medium onion, minced
2 cups diced tomatoes
1 cup (100 g) green beans, cut into 2-in (5-cm) lengths
1 cup (100 g) okra, trimmed and sliced into 1-in ($2^1/2$-cm) pieces
2 cups (150 g) squash or pumpkin, peeled and cubed
2 cups (150 g) eggplants, cut into chunks
8–10 cloves garlic, peeled and minced
2 tablespoons dried shrimp paste, crumbled

1 Sprinkle salt on the bitter gourd and pour over the vinegar. Mix well and set aside for 20 minutes, then drain.

2 Place the pork and water in a saucepan and simmer over low heat for 5 minutes, until pork is almost cooked. Remove pork from the pan and reserve the pork stock. Heat the oil in a frying pan and sauté the pork until lightly browned. Set aside the pork and reserve the pork oil.

3 Arrange the bitter gourd on the bottom of a large casserole or claypot. Add the onions, tomatoes, green beans, okra, squash and eggplants in layers. Sprinkle the garlic over it, then top with the pork and pour in the reserved pork oil.

4 Combine the shrimp paste and the reserved pork stock in a small bowl. Mix well then pour into the casserole or claypot. Simmer for 10–15 minutes or until the vegetables are tender but still crisp.

5 Serve hot with rice.

Serves 4–6
Preparation time: **30 mins**
Cooking time: **25 mins**

Stuffed Grilled Eggplants (Rellenong Talong)

2 lbs (900 g) eggplants
2 tablespoons oil
$^1/_2$ medium onion, minced
6 cloves garlic, minced
10 oz (300 g) ground pork
2 eggs
1 teaspoon salt
$^1/_2$ cup (60 g) flour for dredging
$^1/_2$ cup (125 ml) oil for frying
2 medium tomatoes, diced, to garnish (optional)
2 scallions, chopped, to garnish (optional)

Serves 4–6
Preparation time: **10 mins**
Cooking time: **40 mins**

1 Grill the eggplants under the broiler until soft inside and blackened on the outside, about 10 minutes on each side. Peel off the blackened skins but do not remove stems. Flatten eggplants with the back of a fork into a fan-like shape. Set aside.

2 Heat the 2 tablespoons of oil in a frying pan for 1 minute. Sauté the onions until soft, then add garlic and sauté until fragrant. Add the ground pork and sauté until lightly browned, then set aside.

3 Beat the eggs in a shallow bowl. Dip the flattened eggplants in the beaten eggs. Press some of the cooked pork onto each eggplant with the back of a spoon and season with salt. Dredge each eggplant in flour.

4 Heat the oil in a wok, then fry the eggplants one or two at a time until browned, 3–4 minutes on each side. Remove from pan and drain on paper towels.

5 Garnish with tomatoes and scallions, if desired, and serve.

If using fat Mediterranean eggplants instead of thin Asian eggplants, slice in half before grilling. Grill the eggplants then cut into quarters.

Flatten eggplants with the back of a fork into a fan-like shape.

Spoon some of the cooked pork into each eggplant.

Stir-fried Rice Vermicelli (Pancit Bihon)

1 cup (100 g) small fresh shrimp, peeled (heads and shells reserved)
3 cups (750 ml) water
1/4 cup (60 ml) oil
2 dried Chinese sausages, (see note) thinly sliced
1 small onion, chopped
3–4 cloves garlic, chopped
7 oz (200 g) ground pork
2 cups (150 g) sliced cabbage
1 medium carrot, peeled and thinly sliced
3/4 cup (60 g) sliced green beans
3/4 cup (60 g) snow peas, tops and tails removed
2 chicken bouillon cubes
8 oz (225 g) dried rice vermicelli, soaked in water for 5 minutes and drained
2 tablespoons soy sauce
1 tablespoon hoisin sauce
4 small limes, to serve

Serves 4–6
Preparation time: **20 mins**
Cooking time: **20–25 mins**

1 Boil the reserved shrimp heads and shells in the water for 5 minutes, then mash and strain and discard solids. Set shrimp stock aside.

2 Heat 2 tablespoons of the oil in a wok and sauté the sausage slices. Remove from the wok and set aside.

3 Heat remaining oil in the wok for 1–2 minutes until fragrant and sauté the onions until transparent, 2–3 minutes. Add the garlic and sauté for 1 minute. Sauté the ground pork until lightly browned. Add the sliced cabbage, carrots, green beans and snow peas and stir-fry, until vegetables are almost tender, 1–2 minutes.

4 Pour in the reserved shrimp stock and add the chicken bouillon cubes. Bring to a simmer over low heat. Add the noodles to the wok and stir-fry for 5 minutes. Add the shrimp and reserved sausages. Stir in the soy sauce and hoisin sauce. Simmer the mixture until shrimp are fully cooked, 2–3 minutes, then serve hot. Slice each lime in half and serve with the noodles.

Chinese sausages or lap cheong, are widely available in unrefrigerated packages of various sizes in Asian food shops. Made chiefly of pork, they are similar to salami and have a salty and slightly sweet taste and bright red color. A similar quantity of salami or diced bacon or meat jerky may be substituted.

Cantonese-style Noodles (Pancit Canton)

2 tablespoons oil
1 small onion, minced
2 tablespoons minced garlic
7 oz (200 g) sliced pork
8 oz (250 g) chicken breast or thigh, sliced
1 medium carrot, peeled and julienned
1 cup (100 g) snow peas, tops and tails removed
2 cups (150 g) thinly sliced cabbage
8 oz (225 g) fresh squid, cleaned and thinly sliced into rings or squid balls, deep-fried until lightly browned
1 1/2 cups (375 ml) water
2 chicken or beef bouillon cubes
4 oz (120 g) dried egg noodles (*canton noodles*)
2 tablespoons soy sauce
3 tablespoons butter
6 quail eggs, hard-boiled, peeled and sliced, to garnish (use 3 normal eggs, if unavailable)

Soy Dip
1/4 cup (60 ml) soy sauce
1 tablespoon lime juice

1 Heat the oil in a wok and sauté the onions until transparent, 2–3 minutes. Add garlic and sauté until fragrant, about 1 minute. Add the pork and chicken and sauté until lightly browned, about 2–3 minutes.
2 Add carrots, snow peas, cabbage and squid. Stir-fry over high heat, mixing well. Pour in the water. Add chicken or beef bouillon cubes. Simmer over medium heat for 1 minute, then add noodles and soy sauce.
3 Simmer until almost all the liquid is absorbed and egg noodles are tender, 5–10 minutes. Add the butter and stir until the noodles are evenly coated.
4 To make the Soy Dip, combine the soy sauce and lime juice in a bowl.
5 Garnish noodles with the sliced quail eggs and serve with the Soy Dip.

Serves 6
Preparation time: 30 mins
Cooking time: 20 mins

Shrimp Rice Noodles (Pancit Palabok)

1 lb (450 g) fresh medium shrimp
12 cups (3 liters) water
$1/4$ cup (60 ml) oil
6 tablespoons minced garlic
$1 1/2$ cups (300 g) diced pork
1 cup (200 g) diced pressed tofu (*tokwa*)
2 tablespoons annatto seeds, soaked in 2 tablespoons oil (optional)
2 tablespoons fish sauce
2 tablespoons cornstarch dissolved in $1/4$ cup (60 ml) water
14 oz (400 g) dried rice vermicelli
2 oz (50 g) *chicharon* (see note)
4 scallions, chopped
2 hard-boiled eggs, cut into wedges
8 small limes, to serve

Serves 6–8
Preparation time: 30 mins
Cooking time: 30 mins

1 Peel and devein the shrimp, reserving shells and heads. Simmer the reserved shells and heads in 2 cups (500 ml) water until the water turns orange. Strain into a bowl and press the heads and shells to extract the juice. Reserve the shrimp stock and discard the heads and shells.

2 Simmer the peeled shrimp in 2 cups (500 ml) water, until shrimps turn orange, 2–3 minutes. Drain and set aside.

3 Heat 2 tablespoons of the oil in a wok and sauté garlic until browned. Remove from heat and set aside.

4 Heat remaining oil in a pan and sauté pork until fully cooked. Remove from heat and set aside. In the same pan, sauté the pressed tofu until lightly browned. Set aside.

5 If using annatto seeds, press them in the oil to extract the color. Strain the colored oil into a bowl and set aside.

6 Simmer the shrimp stock in a saucepan, stir in the annatto oil and season with fish sauce. Stir in the cornstarch mixture. Simmer for 3–5 minutes, stirring occasionally, until the liquid thickens.

7 Bring the remaining 8 cups (2 liters) of water to a boil in a stockpot. Drop in the dried rice vermicelli and simmer for 5 minutes or until tender. Drain.

8 Arrange the vermicelli on a serving dish. Pour the reserved shrimp gravy over the noodles. Arrange the cooked pork, firm tofu, shrimp and *chicharon*, if using, on top. Garnish with the reserved garlic, scallions and hard-boiled eggs. Slice each lime in half and serve.

Chicharon, *or deep-fried pork cracklings, are thin pieces of pork rind that are grilled and then deep-fried until crispy. They are sold in packets and are available in Asian grocery stores.*

Noodle Soup with Meat Balls
(Misua with Bola Bola)

1 lb (450 g) ground pork
1 medium carrot, peeled and grated
$^1/_2$ medium onion, minced
1 egg
1 tablespoon flour
$^1/_4$ teaspoon salt, adding extra to taste
$^1/_4$ teaspoon pepper, adding extra to taste
8 cups (2 liters) water
2 chicken bouillon cubes
$3^1/_2$ oz (100 g) dried wheat noodle threads (*misua*)
2 teaspoons fish sauce
$^1/_4$ cup chopped scallions, to garnish (optional)

1 Combine the pork, carrots, onions, egg and flour in a mixing bowl. Season with salt and pepper and mix thoroughly. Scoop out about 1 tablespoon of the meat mixture and shape into a ball. Set aside. Repeat with remaining meat mixture.
2 Bring the water to a boil in a deep pot. Add the pork balls and simmer over medium heat until fully cooked, about 15 minutes.
3 Stir in the bouillon cubes. When cubes dissolve, add the noodles. Season with fish sauce. Simmer for 2–3 minutes over low heat then garnish with scallions, if desired, and serve.

Wheat noodle threads, known as misua *in the Philippines, are very thin noodles made from wheat flour. The dried noodles must be soaked briefly in hot water before use.*

Serves 6
Preparation time: **30 mins**
Cooking time: **15–20 mins**

Chicken and Rice Porridge (Arroz Caldo)

A rice porridge rich with the flavors of chicken broth and ginger, this dish is a favorite on cold, rainy nights.

$^1/_4$ cup (60 ml) olive oil
2 lbs (900 g) chicken pieces (breast, thigh and drumsticks)
$^1/_2$ cup (about 1$^1/_2$ oz/ 40 g) garlic cloves, peeled and crushed
8 cloves (40 g) garlic, minced
$^1/_2$ cup (50 g) thin ginger strips
1$^1/_2$ cups (300 g) uncooked rice
8 cups (2 liters) chicken stock
3 tablespoons fish sauce
$^1/_4$ cup scallions, sliced into thin strips with a vegetable peeler, to garnish
6–8 small limes
Sliced fresh chilies (optional)
2 tablespoons soy sauce (optional)

1 Heat 2 tablespoons of oil in a casserole. Add the chicken pieces and stir-fry until lightly browned, then remove with a slotted spoon and set aside.

2 In the same casserole, sauté half of the minced garlic until lightly browned. Remove the garlic from the casserole and set aside.

3 Pour in the remaining oil. Sauté the ginger and remaining garlic. Add the rice and stir until coated with oil. Pour in the chicken stock. Add the chicken and fish sauce. Simmer until rice and chicken are fully cooked, about 40 minutes. The mixture should have a soupy consistency when fully cooked.

4 Spoon into individual serving bowls and garnish with the reserved fried garlic and scallions. Serve with limes and sliced fresh chilies with soy sauce, if desired.

Serves 6
Preparation time: **10 mins**
Cooking time: **35 mins**

Cuban-style Rice (Arroz a la Cubana)

A complex dish with various flavors, Arroz a la Cubana combines the richness of meat with the sweetness of fried plantains and raisins. Eggs fried sunny side up make this a very filling, one-dish meal.

$1/2$ cup (125 ml) oil
1 medium potato, peeled and diced
1 lb (450 g) plantains, peeled and sliced lengthwise
6–8 eggs
1 small onion, diced
4 cloves garlic, peeled and minced
8 oz (225 g) ground pork
$1^1/2$ teaspoons salt
8 oz (225 g) ground beef
$1/2$ teaspoon Worcestershire sauce
$3/4$ cup (120 g) fresh or frozen green peas
$1/4$ cup (45 g) raisins
4–6 cups cooked rice

Serves 6–8
Preparation time: **10 mins**
Cooking time: **30 mins**

1 Heat 2 tablespoons of the oil in a wok or skillet over medium heat and sauté the potatoes until just tender, about 10 minutes. Remove from the wok and set aside. In the same wok, add another 2 tablespoons oil and fry the sliced plantains until lightly browned on both sides and tender. Remove and drain on paper towels and set aside.

2 Heat another 2 tablespoons of the oil and fry the eggs, sunny side up, adding more oil if necessary. Remove the eggs when cooked and set aside.

3 Heat the remaining oil in a large skillet or casserole and sauté the onions and garlic. Add the ground pork and stir-fry until browned. Season with $1/2$ teaspoon of the salt.

4 Add the ground beef and stir-fry until the beef browns. Season with $1/2$ teaspoon salt and stir in the Worcestershire sauce.

5 Mix in green peas and stir well. Add the reserved potatoes and raisins. Season with remaining salt. Stir-fry for about 5 minutes until all ingredients are well mixed.

6 To serve, spoon the ground meat mixture into a serving platter. Add the cooked eggs and plantains on top and serve with plain rice.

Fried Rice with Shrimp and Chinese Sausage (Morisqueta Tostada)

This dish is typical of what is known in the Philippines as *comida china*: Chinese dishes with Spanish names. The Spaniards and the Chinese were a strong presence in the Philippines from the 16th to the early 20th century. When the Chinese opened the first noodle shop restaurants known as *panciterias*, Spanish was the language of commerce, hence the dishes all acquired Spanish names.

$1/2$ cup (125 ml) water
2 Chinese sausages
$1/4$ cup (60 ml) oil
2 eggs, lightly beaten
1 medium onion, minced
4 cloves garlic, peeled and minced
8 oz (225 g) fresh medium shrimp, peeled and deveined
6 cups (900 g) cooked white rice (leftover rice is best; if freshly cooked, allow rice to cool before frying)
$1^1/2$ tablepoons soy sauce
3 scallions, chopped, to garnish
Few sprigs coriander leaves (cilantro), to garnish

Serves 6
Preparation time: **5 mins**
Cooking time: **30 mins**

1 Pour the water into a frying pan and simmer the sausages over low heat until the water evaporates, 5–10 minutes. Continue to fry the sausages until fully cooked, turning frequently so the sausages do not burn. Remove the sausages from the pan and slice thinly. Set aside to cool.

2 Heat 1 tablespoon of the oil in a pan and scramble the eggs. Remove the scrambled eggs from the pan and set aside.

3 Heat the remaining oil in a wok. Sauté the onions until transparent, 2–3 minutes. Add garlic and sauté until fragrant. Add the shrimp and stir-fry until pink, 1–2 minutes.

4 Immediately add the cooked rice, reserved sausages and scrambled eggs. Season with soy sauce. Stir-fry until rice becomes evenly browned. Garnish with scallions and coriander leaves.

Chinese sausages, or lap cheong, *are widely available in unrefrigerated packages of various sizes in Asian food shops and well-stocked supermarkets. Made chiefly of pork, they are similar to salami and have a salty and slightly sweet taste. A similar quantity of diced bacon can be substituted if unavailable.*

Seafood Paella

Paella originated in Valencia, Spain, where it remains a popular dish. In the Philippines, which was a Spanish colony for 300 years, this rice dish has evolved to suit local tastes and preferences.

1 lb (450 g) medium clams in the shell
8 oz (225 g) small squid, ink sacs, heads and tentacles removed
$1/4$ cup (60 ml) oil
2 Spanish sausages, thinly sliced
1 medium onion, minced
1 medium tomato, diced
1 teaspoon paprika
Few saffron threads or $1/4$ teaspoon saffron powder
6 cups ($1 1/2$ liters) warm chicken stock
3 cups (600 g) uncooked white, short grain rice
1 lb (450 g) fresh medium shrimp
1 green bell pepper, thinly sliced
1 red bell pepper, thinly sliced
2 hard-boiled eggs, peeled and cut into wedges
2 lemons, cut into wedges (optional)

1 Scrub and rinse the clam shells thoroughly. Steam clams for 3–4 minutes until they open slightly. Discard any shells that remain closed and set aside steamed clams. Slice squid into $1/2$-in (1-cm) rings and set aside.

2 Heat 2 tablespoons of the oil in a large skillet or casserole. Cook the sausages until browned, about 2 minutes on each side. Remove from skillet and set aside.

3 Heat remaining oil over medium heat and sauté the onions until fragrant, 1–2 minutes. Add the tomato and stir-fry for 2 minutes. Reduce heat to low and add paprika. Stir-fry for 1 minute. Add the saffron and warm chicken stock and bring to a simmer.

4 Spread the rice evenly in the skillet or casserole. Simmer for about 10 minutes, stirring occasionally, then add the shrimp. When shrimp are cooked, remove from pan and set aside. Simmer for another five minutes then add squid rings and bell peppers. Remove squid rings as soon as they are cooked, about one minute. Set aside.

5 Allow rice to simmer until liquid has been absorbed and rice is slightly dry, about 30 minutes. Remove from heat. Top with clams, Spanish sausages, shrimp, squid and hard-boiled eggs. Serve in a serving platter with lemon wedges, if desired.

Serves 6–8
Preparation time: 25 mins
Cooking time: 40 mins

Sweet and Sour Fish
(Escabeche)

1 red snapper or grouper (about 2 lbs/900 g), cleaned and scaled or 1 lb (450 g) fish steaks
$1/_2$ cup (65 g) flour mixed with $1/_2$ teaspoon salt, for dredging
125 ml ($1/_2$ cup) oil
Few sprigs fresh coriander leaves (cilantro), to garnish

Sweet and Sour Sauce
$1/_2$ cup (100 g) superfine sugar
$1/_2$ cup (125 ml) vinegar
$1/_2$ cup (125 ml) water
3 tablespoons tomato ketchup
1 small carrot, peeled and thinly sliced
1 medium green bell pepper, thinly sliced
1 medium red bell pepper, thinly sliced
1 medium cucumber, peeled, halved lengthwise and thinly sliced
$1/_2$ tablespoon cornstarch dissolved in 2 tablespoons water

1 Make 3–4 diagonal slits along each side of the fish and dredge in flour. Heat the oil in a wok and fry the fish for 7–8 minutes on each side, or until completely cooked. Remove from pan and drain on paper towels.
2 To make the Sweet and Sour Sauce, combine the sugar, vinegar, water and tomato ketchup in a saucepan. Add carrots, cook for 4–5 minutes, then add bell peppers and cucumber. Simmer, without stirring, for another 3 minutes or until vegetables are just tender. Stir in cornstarch mixture and simmer until sauce thickens. Remove from heat.
3 Place the fish on a serving platter. Pour the Sweet and Sour Sauce over the fish. Arrange vegetables around fish and garnish with fresh coriander leaves.

Serves 4–6
Preparation time: **15 mins**
Cooking time: **25 mins**

Shrimp in Sweet and Sour Sauce (Camaron Rebosado)

2 cups (250 g) flour
2 teaspoons salt
2 lbs (900 g) medium shrimp, peeled and deveined, tails intact
2 eggs, lightly beaten
1 cup (250 ml) oil

Sweet and Sour Sauce
$1/2$ cup (100 g) sugar
$1/2$ teaspoon salt
$1/4$ cup (60 ml) tomato ketchup
$1/2$ cup (125 ml) vinegar
2 tablespoons cornstarch dissolved in 1 cup (250 ml) water

1 Combine the flour and salt in a mixing bowl. Dredge each shrimp in the flour mixture, dip in the egg, then dredge in flour again.
2 Heat the oil in a wok over medium heat. Deep-fry shrimp in batches until lightly browned, 2–3 minutes. Drain on paper towels.
3 To make the Sweet and Sour Sauce, mix the sugar, salt, ketchup and vinegar in a saucepan. Simmer over low heat. Stir in the cornstarch mixture.
4 Continue simmering, stirring occasionally, until the sauce thickens. Pour the Sweet and Sour Sauce over the cooked shrimp or serve as a dip.

Serves 6
Preparation time: **40 mins**
Cooking time: **40 mins–1 hour**

Stuffed Crabs (Rellenong Alimasag)

The stuffing contains fresh crabmeat sautéed with garlic, onions and tomatoes, which give it added flavor. You may steam the crab ahead and pry the meat from the shells. Refrigerate the crabmeat until ready to cook.

4 lbs (2 kgs) small fresh crabs (4–6 crabs)
1/3 cup (80 ml) oil
1 small onion, minced
3–4 cloves garlic, peeled and minced
2–3 small tomatoes, diced
1/4 teaspoon salt, adding extra to taste
1/4 teaspoon pepper, adding extra to taste
1 egg, lightly beaten
2 tablespoons cornstarch
2 tablespoons bread-crumbs

Serves 4–6
Preparation time: **10 mins**
Cooking time: **30 mins**

1 Steam the crabs until cooked, about 10 minutes. Set aside to cool then open the crabs and discard the spongy gray matter inside the shell. Scoop out the flesh and set aside. Reserve the shells and claws.

2 Heat 2 tablespoons of the oil in a frying pan and sauté the onions for 1 minute. Add the garlic and sauté until fragrant, 1–2 minutes. Add the tomatoes and sauté until tender. Add the reserved crabmeat and stir-fry. Season with salt and pepper and remove from the heat.

3 Spoon the crabmeat mixture back into each of the shells. Brush lightly with egg, then dust lightly with cornstarch and breadcrumbs.

4 Heat remaining oil in a pan over medium heat. Cook crab shells in the hot oil, stuffed side facing down, until a light brown crust forms on the stuffing. Remove from heat and serve with the reserved claws, if desired.

You may make these using 10 oz (300 g) freshly cooked crab meat rather than whole crabs. Follow the recipe from step 2 onwards. Shape the crab mixture into patties, dust with cornstarch and breadcrumbs then fry.

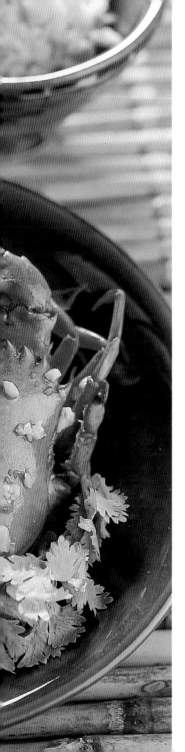

Fresh Braised Crabs with Garlic (Adobong Alimango)

3 lbs (1½ kgs) fresh crabs
¼ cup (60 ml) oil
8 cloves (40 g) garlic, minced
1½ cups (375 ml) water
⅓ cup (80 ml) lime juice
¼ teaspoon salt, adding extra to taste
¼ teaspoon pepper, adding extra to taste
4 small limes, to garnish (optional)
2 sprigs coriander leaves (cilantro), to garnish (optional)

1 Cut the crabs into half and discard the spongy gray matter in the shell. Remove the yellow crab tissue and set aside. Heat the oil in a wok and sauté the garlic until fragrant, about 1 minute. Add the crabs and stir-fry until pink.
2 Mix the reserved crab tissue with water and lime juice to form a smooth mixture. Pour into the wok with crabs and season with salt and pepper. Simmer over medium heat until crabs turn red, about 10 minutes. Serve garnished with limes and coriander leaves, if desired.

Serves 4
Preparation time: **10 mins**
Cooking time: **15 mins**

Fried Fish Steaks (Fish Sarciado)

4 Spanish mackerel steaks
(about 1 lb/450 g)
2¹/₂ tablespoons lime
juice
5 tablespoons olive oil
8–10 cloves garlic,
peeled and crushed
1 large onion, minced
1 medium tomato, diced
2 tablespoons fish sauce
1 cup (250 ml) water

Serves 4
Preparation time: **5 mins**
 + 30 mins marinating
Cooking time: **15 mins**

1 Marinate the fish steaks in lime juice for 30 minutes. Heat 3 tablespoons of the olive oil in a frying pan and sauté the fish steaks until fully cooked, about 5 minutes on each side. Remove fish steaks from the frying pan and set aside.

2 Heat the remaining oil in a separate pan and sauté the garlic, onions and tomatoes, until tender. Stir in the fish sauce and water. Simmer until most of the liquid has been absorbed.

3 Spoon the onion and tomato mixture over the cooked fish steaks. Serve with rice.

Pork Stewed in Sweet Vinegar Soy (Humba)

$^1/_2$ cup (100 g) dark brown sugar
2 cups (500 ml) water
$^1/_4$ cup (60 ml) soy sauce
$^3/_4$ cup (200 ml) vinegar
2 lbs (900 g) pork shoulder, cut into chunks
3–4 cloves garlic, minced
1 bay leaf

1 Combine the sugar, water, soy sauce and vinegar in a bowl and stir well. Transfer to a casserole and add the pork, garlic and bay leaf.
2 Bring to a boil over high heat, then simmer over low heat until pork is tender, about 35 minutes.
3 Discard the bay leaf and serve meat with rice. Spoon over the sauce.

Serves 6
Preparation time: **5 mins**
Cooking time: **40 mins**

Chicken and Vegetable Stew
(Chicken Cocido)

1/4 cup (60 ml) oil
2 Spanish sausages, sliced on the diagonal
1 medium onion, minced
8–10 cloves garlic, minced
2 lbs (900 g) chicken pieces (breast, thighs and drumsticks)
2 cups (500 ml) water
2 medium carrots, peeled and thinly sliced
2 potatoes, peeled and cut into chunks
2–3 cups thickly sliced plantains
2 cups (500 ml) canned tomato sauce
1 medium head green cabbage, quartered

Dip
1 cup (250 ml) fish sauce
1/2 cup (125 ml) lime juice

1 To make the Dip, mix the fish sauce and lime juice then divide into 4–6 equal portions and set aside.
2 Heat the oil in a large casserole and sauté the sausages until browned, about 2 minutes on each side. Remove sausages from the pan and set aside. Sauté the onions in the oil for 1 minute, then add garlic and sauté until fragrant, 1–2 minutes. Add chicken and sauté until lightly browned on all sides, about 10 minutes. Pour in the water and bring to a boil over high heat. Reduce heat to low and simmer for 10 minutes.
3 Add carrots, cook for 7–8 minutes, then add potatoes, plantains and reserved sausages.
4 Stir in tomato sauce and simmer until the chicken, vegetables and plantains are tender. Add the cabbage and heat through until cabbage leaves are just tender and chicken pieces are completely cooked.
5 Serve with rice and the Dip.

Serves 4–6
Preparation time: **15 mins**
Cooking time: **40–50 mins**

Chicken Pot Pie (Chicken Pastel)

1 lb (450 g) boneless
chicken meat
2$^1/_2$ tablespoons lime
juice
$^1/_4$ cup (60 ml) soy sauce
2 tablespoons oil
2 Spanish sausages, sliced
2 oz (50 g) butter
1 medium onion, minced
3–4 cloves garlic, minced
1 cup (250 ml) water
1 medium carrot, peeled
and diced
2 medium potatoes,
peeled and diced
$^1/_4$ cup (60 ml) white
wine
2 hot dogs or Wiener
sausages (140 g), thinly
sliced
1 cup (200 g) canned
button mushrooms,
drained and sliced
1$^1/_4$ cups (200 g) fresh
or frozen green peas
$^1/_4$ teaspoon salt
$^1/_4$ teaspoon pepper
2 tablespoons cornstarch
$^1/_4$ cup (60 ml) water
3 hard-boiled eggs
1 egg yolk, lightly beaten

Pie Crust
1$^1/_4$ cups (160 g) flour
$^1/_4$ teaspoon salt
$^1/_4$ cup (60 g) chilled
butter
2 tablespoons (50 g)
chilled solid vegetable
shortening
3–4 tablespoons iced
water

1 To make the Pie Crust, sift together flour and salt in a bowl. Using a pastry blender or two knives, cut the butter and shortening into the flour until mixture resembles coarse breadcrumbs. Sprinkle water over the mixture, gathering the crumbs until they form a ball. Sprinkle flour on waxed paper and wrap dough in the paper. Chill in a refrigerator for 30 minutes.

2 Cut the chicken pieces into bite-sized chunks and marinate in lime juice and soy sauce for 20 minutes.

3 Heat the oil in a casserole until hot. Sauté Spanish sausages until browned, about 2 minutes on each side. Remove the sausages and set aside.

4 Add butter to the casserole. When butter melts, sauté onions until transparent, 2–3 minutes. Add garlic and sauté until fragrant. Add chicken (discarding marinade) and sauté over low heat until lightly browned.

5 Stir in water and simmer for 10 minutes. Add carrots and potatoes. Simmer for 15 minutes until chicken, carrots and potatoes are almost tender. Stir in white wine, sausages, mushrooms, peas and reserved Spanish sausages. Add the salt and pepper and mix.

6 Preheat oven to 375°F (190°C). Blend cornstarch and water in a small bowl until smooth and stir into casserole. Simmer until liquid thickens, about 5 minutes.

7 Spoon the filling into a baking dish. Slice the hard-boiled eggs and place on top of the filling.

8 Sprinkle flour onto a smooth work surface. Roll out the chilled pie dough until it is 3 mm ($^1/_8$ in) thick and forms a circle, 5 cm (2 in) larger than the baking dish.

9 Cover the baking dish with the Pie Crust and brush the crust with egg yolk. Fold the dough over the edges of the baking dish and flute or decorate the edges. Make slits on the surface of the crust to let steam escape

10 Alternatively, cut the chilled dough into long strips and arrange to form a lattice pattern on top of the filling, as shown in the photograph. Bake for about 30 minutes or until crust is golden brown.

Serves 6–8
Preparation time: **30 mins + 30 mins chilling time**
Cooking time: **1 hour 10 mins**

Chicken and Pork Adobo

2 lbs (900 g) pork belly or shoulder, cut into chunks
1 chicken (3 lbs/1$^1/_2$ kg), cut into serving portions
$^1/_2$ cup (40 g) minced garlic
1$^1/_2$ cups (375 ml) vinegar
1$^1/_2$ cups (375 ml) water
1 bay leaf (optional)
2 tablespoons salt
$^1/_2$ cup (125 ml) oil
$^1/_4$ cup (60 ml) soy sauce
4 medium tomatoes, diced (optional)

Serves 8–10
Preparation time: **10 mins**
Cooking time: **1 hour**

1 Put the pork and chicken in a large casserole. Sprinkle garlic over the pork and chicken. Combine vinegar and water and pour into the casserole. (Do not use an aluminum casserole as the aluminum will react with the vinegar.)
2 Bring to a boil without stirring, then simmer over low heat and add the bay leaf, if using. Add salt and simmer until the meat is tender, about 30 minutes. Remove the meat from the casserole and reserve any liquid.
3 Heat the oil in a wok and cook the pork and chicken in batches until browned. Remove the pork and chicken and place in a serving dish.
4 Mix the soy sauce and reserved liquid. Pour over the meat. Serve with hot rice and chopped tomatoes, if desired, and Green Mango and Tomato Relish (see page 9).

Beef Shanks with Vegetables (Pochero)

2–3 cups thickly sliced plantains
2 tablespoons oil
2 Spanish sausages, thinly sliced
2 lbs (900 g) boneless beef shanks
8 cups (2 liters) beef stock or water
2 medium potatoes, peeled and cubed
³/₄ cup (100 g) chickpeas
1 head green cabbage, quartered
2 tablespoons fish sauce

Dip
1 cup (250 ml) fish sauce
¹/₂ cup (125 ml) lime juice

1 Mix the Dip ingredients then divide into 6–8 equal portions and set aside.
2 Slice the plantains into thick pieces then set aside.
3 Heat the oil in a frying pan and fry the sausages for 2 minutes on each side or until browned. Set aside.
4 Bring the beef shanks and beef stock to a boil in a stockpot over high heat, then reduce heat to low and simmer for 1¹/₂ hours, or until beef is just tender. Add water if needed to prevent the stock from drying out.
5 Add the potatoes and the plantains then simmer for 15 minutes more. Add the chickpeas and reserved sausages and simmer for another 5 minutes.
6 Add cabbage and season with fish sauce. Simmer until cabbage is just tender, 2–3 minutes. Serve with rice and Dip.

Serves 6–8
Preparation time: **15 mins**
Cooking time: **2 hours**

Stewed Pork (Estofado)

³/₄ cup (150 g) sugar
1 cup (250 ml) vinegar
¹/₂ cup (125 ml) soy sauce
1 cup (250 ml) water
¹/₄ cup (60 ml) oil
8 cloves (40 g) garlic, minced
2 lbs (900 g) boneless pork shoulder, cut into chunks
1 bay leaf
1 medium carrot, thinly sliced
2–3 cups thickly sliced plantains
4 buns or *pan de sal*, each quartered (optional)
1 scallion, cut into thin strips with a vegetable peeler
  to garnish (optional)

1 Combine the sugar, vinegar, soy sauce and water in a mixing bowl then set aside.
2 Heat 2 tablespoons of the oil in a wok or casserole. Fry the garlic until browned then set aside.
3 Pour in the remaining oil, add pork and sauté until medium brown. Pour in the reserved vinegar mixture. Bring to a boil, then simmer over low heat. (Do not stir until the vinegar mixture boils, otherwise the meat will taste raw.) Add bay leaf and simmer for 20 minutes or until pork is tender.
4 Add the carrots and simmer for 5 minutes. Add the plantains. After 5 minutes, stir in the buns or *pan de sal*, if desired. Simmer until the pork is fully cooked and plantains and carrots are tender, about 5–10 minutes. Garnish with scallions, if desired.
5 Serve with rice or additional buns or *pan de sal*.

Pan de sal *is the national bread of the Philippines, usually made with salt, yeast, sugar and flour and shaped into a bun. If* pan de sal *is not available, it may be substituted with any bun or bread.*

Serves 6
Preparation time: **5–10 mins**
Cooking time: **45 mins**

Grilled Marinated Pork
(Inihaw na Baboy)

2 lbs (900 g) pork belly or pork ribs
$^1/_2$ cup (40 g) minced garlic
$^1/_2$ cup (125 ml) 7-Up or Sprite
$^1/_2$ cup (125 ml) vinegar
2 tablespoons sugar
$^1/_4$ teaspoon freshly ground black pepper, adding extra
   to taste
1 portion Papaya Relish (see page 12)

Vinegar Soy Dip
1 medium onion, minced
1 cup (250 ml) vinegar
$^1/_2$ cup (125 ml) soy sauce
$^1/_4$ teaspoon freshly ground black pepper, adding extra
   to taste
1 red chili, sliced (optional)

1 Slice pork belly lengthwise into thick strips. If using pork ribs, separate or slice across.
2 Combine garlic, Sprite or 7-Up, vinegar, sugar and pepper in a bowl. Pour over the pork. Cover and marinate for 3–4 hours in the refrigerator.
3 Drain the pork and discard marinade. Heat a grill or broiler to medium. Cook the pork under the pre-heated broiler or over a barbecue grill until browned and cooked through, about 10–15 minutes on each side.
4 To make the Vinegar Soy Dip, combine the onions, vinegar, soy sauce and ground black pepper in a bowl and stir. For a spicier dip, add the sliced chilies or more black pepper to taste.
5 Serve the grilled pork with Vinegar Soy Dip, Papaya Relish and cooked white rice.

Makes 4–6 Servings
Preparation time: 5 mins + 1 hour for marinating
Cooking time: 30 mins

Sweet Pineapple-cured Pork (Pork Tocino)

1 lb (450 g) pork shoulder
$^1/_2$ cup (125 ml) oil
2 scallions, cut into thin strips
2 medium tomatoes, thinly sliced, to garnish
$^1/_2$ medium cucumber, halved lengthwise then thinly sliced, to garnish

Marinade
$^3/_4$ cup (150 g) dark brown sugar
1 cup (250 ml) canned pineapple juice
$^1/_4$ teaspoon freshly ground black pepper, adding extra to taste

1 To make the Marinade, combine the sugar, pineapple juice and ground black pepper in a bowl. Cut the pork into thin slices and place in a mixing bowl or plate. Pour over the Marinade and mix thoroughly. Cover and marinate in the refrigerator for a few hours or overnight.

2 Heat half of the oil in a skillet over medium heat. Drain the marinated pork slices and fry in batches, adding more oil as needed.

3 Garnish with scallions and serve with rice, sliced tomatoes, cucumbers, and Green Mango and Tomato Relish (see page 9).

Serves 4–6
Preparation time: **10 mins + overnight marinating**
Cooking time: **20–25 mins**

Deep-fried Pork (Lechon Kawali)

2 lbs (900 g) pork belly
  with skin
1 medium onion, sliced
8 cups (2 liters) water
  for boiling
Oil for deep-frying
$\frac{1}{2}$ cup water for sprin-
  kling
Garlic Vinegar Dip or
  Lechon Sauce (see
  page 7)

Serves 6–8
Preparation time: **5 mins**
Cooking time: **1 hour**

1 Place pork belly and onions in a stockpot, add water to cover and bring to a boil over high heat. Lower heat to medium and simmer for about 45 minutes or until pork is just tender (not too soft or it won't be crispy when fried). Drain pork and pat dry with paper towels.
2 Heat the oil over high heat in a large wok or frying pan until very hot. Carefully put the pork belly in the oil, skin-side up. Reduce heat to medium and deep-fry pork until skin is lightly browned, 10–15 minutes.
3 Sprinkle some water on the skin of the pork. This will form blisters on the pork skin and make it crispy. Continue cooking until the skin is golden brown, 10–15 minutes. Remove from the wok or pan and drain on paper towels. Slice and serve with Garlic Vinegar Dip (see page 7) or with Lechon Sauce (see page 7).

Diced Pork in Tomato Sauce
(Menudo)

This easy-to-prepare dish is ideal for a weekday dinner. The pork, potatoes and carrots all cook very quickly and the tomato sauce adds valuable nutrients, such as lycopene, to the dish.

2 tablespoons oil
1 small onion, diced
1 tablespoon minced garlic
2 lbs (900 g) pork shoulder, cut into bite-sized pieces
1 large potato, diced
2 medium carrots, diced
1 cup (250 ml) water
2 tablespoons soy sauce, adding extra to taste
2 cups (500 ml) canned tomato sauce
2 tablespoons lime juice

1 Heat the oil in a large frying pan or wok and sauté the onions for about 1 minute. Add the garlic and sauté for 1 minute.
2 Add the pork and stir-fry until lightly browned. Add the potatoes and carrots and stir-fry for 2–3 minutes.
3 Pour in water and simmer 15 minutes. Stir in soy sauce, tomato sauce and lime juice. Mix thoroughly.
4 Bring to a boil, then immediately lower heat. Simmer until pork is cooked through and potatoes and carrots are tender, about 15 minutes.
5 Serve warm with rice or bread.

Serves 6
Preparation time: **10 mins**
Cooking time: **35 mins**

Filipino Sausage (Longganisa)

$1^1/_2$ lbs (650 g) ground pork
3 tablespoons dark brown sugar
2 teaspoons salt
$^1/_4$ teaspoon freshly ground black pepper, adding extra
  to taste
2 tablespoons crushed garlic
1 tablespoon annatto seeds
$^1/_4$ cup (60 ml) vinegar
$^1/_2$ cup (125 ml) oil
2 scallions, cut into thin strips with a vegetable peeler,
  to garnish (optional)
2 medium tomatoes, diced (optional)
1 portion Garlic Vinegar Dip (see page 7)

1 Combine the ground pork, sugar, salt, pepper and garlic in a mixing bowl.
2 Combine the annatto seeds and vinegar in a separate bowl. Press on the annatto seeds with the back of a spoon to extract the color. Strain the colored vinegar into the pork mixture and mix thoroughly.
3 Shape the pork mixture into thin 4-in (10-cm) lengths and wrap in small pieces of waxed paper. Chill for 2–3 hours in the refrigerator, until firm.
4 Heat the oil over high heat in a wok or skillet. Unwrap the pork mixture and fry in batches in hot oil until fully cooked. Drain on paper towels.
5 Garnish with scallions, if desired, and serve with rice and tomatoes or Garlic Vinegar Dip. If not cooking immediately, store the sausages in the freezer.

Makes 18–20 sausages
Preparation time: **30 mins + 2 hours chilling**
Cooking time: **30 mins**

Chicken in Tomato Sauce
(Fritada)

3 tablespoons olive oil
1 small onion, minced
3–4 cloves garlic, minced
2 lbs (900 g) chicken pieces (breast, thighs
   and drumsticks)
1 cup (250 g) crushed canned tomatoes
1 cup (250 ml) water
1 bay leaf
$^1/_4$ cup (60 ml) olive oil
1 lb (450 g) potatoes, peeled and cut into chunks
1 red or green bell pepper, cut into thin strips
$^2/_3$ cup (85 g) pitted green olives
$1^1/_4$ cups (200 g) fresh or frozen green peas
$^1/_4$ teaspoon salt, adding extra to taste
$^1/_4$ teaspoon pepper, adding extra to taste

1 Heat 3 tablespoons of oil in a casserole. Sauté
onions until transparent, 2–3 minutes, then add garlic and sauté until fragrant, 1–2 minutes. Stir-fry the
chicken pieces until evenly browned. Pour in crushed
tomatoes and water. Add the bay leaf and bring to a
boil, then simmer until chicken is just tender, about
20 minutes.
2 In a frying pan or wok, stir-fry the potatoes in
$^1/_4$ cup (60 ml) olive oil over medium heat until
browned on all sides, about 15 minutes.
3 Add the fried potatoes, bell peppers, green peas and
olives and simmer until chicken is tender, 5–10 minutes. Season with salt and pepper. Remove the bay
leaf before serving.

Serves 6
Preparation time: **15 mins**
Cooking time: **30–40 mins**

Flavorful Oxtail Stew (Kare-Kare)

2 lbs (900 g) oxtail, sliced
1 lb (450 g) stewing beef, cut into chunks
18 cups (4$^1/_2$ liters) water
2 tablespoons oil
1 medium onion, diced
3–4 cloves garlic, peeled and minced
$^1/_2$ cup (about 3$^1/_2$ oz/ 100 g) thinly sliced-banana heart (optional)
1 eggplant, thinly sliced
1 cup (100 g) sliced green beans
2 tablespoons annatto seeds
$^1/_2$ cup dry roasted peanuts, finely ground (see note)
$^1/_2$ cup (100 g) uncooked rice, dry roasted and finely ground (see note)
1 tablespoon shrimp paste

Serves 8
Preparation time: **30 mins**
Cooking time: **2 hours**

1 Clean the oxtail and beef thoroughly. In a stockpot, boil the oxtail and beef in 6 cups (1$^1/_2$ liters) of the water for about 10 minutes. Drain and discard the water. Pour the remaining water into the stockpot. Bring to a boil then simmer over low heat until meat is tender, about 1$^1/_2$ hours.

2 Remove the meat from the pot, set aside and reserve the stock.

3 Heat the oil in a casserole and sauté onions until transparent, 2–3 minutes. Add garlic and sauté until fragrant, 1–2 minutes. Pour in 4 cups (1 liter) of the reserved stock. Add the banana heart, if using, bring to a boil and simmer for 5 minutes or until just tender. Add the eggplant and green beans and simmer until just tender.

4 Soak the annatto seeds in $^1/_4$ cup (60 ml) of the reserved stock. Strain the liquid, pour into the casserole or pot and mix well. Stir in the ground peanuts and rice grains to thicken the liquid then add the meat.

5 Blend the shrimp paste with $^1/_4$ cup (60 ml) of the remaining stock, pour into the casserole and stir. Simmer for another 5 minutes or until heated through. Serve with rice and additional shrimp paste.

Dry roast the peanuts and uncooked rice separately in a skillet over medium heat, stirring continuously until evenly browned. Grind in a mortar and pestle or blend in a food processor until fine.

Stuffed Beef Roll (Morcon)

3 lbs (1¹/₂ kg) thinly sliced top round or London broil beef steak
1–2 pork or beef frankfurters or hot dogs
3–6 slices sweet pickles or pickled gherkins
1–2 hard-boiled eggs, quartered
¹/₂ medium carrot, sliced into 2-in (5-cm) strips
Flour for dusting
¹/₄ cup (60 ml) oil
1 cup (250 ml) water
2 medium tomatoes, seeded and diced
¹/₄ teaspoon salt, adding extra to taste
¹/₄ teaspoon pepper, adding extra to taste

Marinade
4 tablespoons lime juice
¹/₄ cup (60 ml) soy sauce

1 To prepare the Marinade, combine the lime juice and soy sauce in a mixing bowl. Pour over the beef and marinate for 30 minutes. Drain beef and reserve the Marinade.

2 Spread beef on a clean, dry surface. If the sheet of beef is too thick, slice it in half. Place 1 frankfurter, 2–3 pickles or gherkins, 3–4 egg slices and 2 carrot strips on each sheet of beef. Roll the beef, enclosing the fillings. Tie the beef with a string.

3 Dust the beef lightly with flour. Heat the oil in a casserole or frying pan and fry the beef until evenly browned. Pour in the water, tomatoes and reserved Marinade. Simmer over low heat until beef is fully cooked and tender, about 1–1¹/₂ hours. Add more water if needed to prevent the gravy from drying up.

4 Remove beef from casserole and reserve the liquid. Set aside to cool for a few minutes then slice into thick serving pieces. Discard the strings.

5 Strain the reserved liquid and serve as a sauce with the beef.

Serves 6–8
Preparation time: **45 mins**
Cooking time: **1¹/₂ hours**

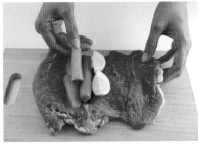

Place the items in a line in the center of the beef.

Roll the beef and tie with string.

Sirloin Steak Filipino-style (Bistek Tagalog)

1 lb (450 g) beef sirloin,
thinly sliced
$^1/_2$ cup (125 ml) lime
juice
$^1/_4$ cup (60 ml) oil
1 medium onion, sliced
into rings
$^1/_4$ cup (60 ml) soy
sauce
$^1/_2$ cup (125 ml) water

Fried Potato Wedges

1 lb (450 g) potatoes,
peeled and cut into
wedges
Oil for deep-frying

1 Marinate the beef in half of the lime juice for
30 minutes.

2 Deep-fry the potato wedges in oil over high heat in
a deep saucepan or wok until golden brown.

3 Heat the oil in a frying pan and sauté the onion
until lightly browned. Set aside.

4 Drain the marinated beef slices and reserve the lime
juice. Sauté the beef in the same frying pan for
1–2 minutes on each side. Combine the remaining
lime juice, soy sauce and water. Pour into the frying
pan with the reserved lime juice.

5 Return the reserved onion rings to the pan and
simmer for 1–2 minutes. Serve hot with fried potato
wedges and rice.

Serves 4
Preparation time: **5 mins + 30 mins marinating**
Cooking time: **15 mins**

Rich Beef Stew (Caldereta)

This dish is a favorite at town fiestas. Long, slow simmering makes the beef tender, while the Spanish sausages, peas and olives add richness to the taste.

3 tablespoons oil
1 1/2 lbs (650 g) stewing beef, cut into chunks
1 medium onion, sliced into rings
6 cups (1 1/2 liters) water
10 oz (300 g) pork liver
2 Spanish sausages, thinly sliced
3/4 cup (60 g) minced garlic
1 1/3 cups (330 ml) canned tomato sauce
1/3 cup (80 ml) vinegar
1 cup (125 g) grated Cheddar cheese
2 tablespoons sugar
1/4 teaspoon salt, adding extra to taste
1/4 teaspoon pepper, adding extra to taste
2 medium potatoes, peeled and cubed
2 medium carrots, sliced
1 red bell pepper, thinly sliced
1 cup (160 g) fresh or frozen green peas
1/2 cup (100 g) green or black olives

1 Heat 2 tablespoons of the oil in a large casserole or wok and sauté the beef until evenly browned. Place the beef and oil in a stockpot. Add the onions and pour in the water. Bring to a boil, then reduce heat to low and simmer.

2 Meanwhile, grill the pork liver under a broiler until it is half cooked, about 7–8 minutes. Remove from the grill and chop finely.

3 In a large saucepan, heat remaining oil and sauté the Spanish sausages until browned, about 2 minutes on each side. Remove from the pan and set aside. Sauté the garlic in the same oil until fragrant. Stir in the liver, tomato sauce and vinegar. Add the cheese, sugar, salt and pepper. Mix thoroughly and simmer 5 minutes, stirring occasionally, to form a smooth mixture.

4 Pour the liver mixture into the simmering beef in the casserole. Stir to combine mixture well with the liquid. Simmer the beef for 30 minutes.

5 Add the potatoes and carrots and simmer over low heat until beef, potatoes and carrots are tender and the sauce thickens, about 30 more minutes.

6 Stir in the reserved Spanish sausages, bell peppers, green peas and olives, and heat through. Serve hot with rice.

Serves 6–8
Preparation time: **15 mins**
Cooking time: **1 hour 30 mins**

Iced Fruit Mix (Halo-Halo)

The literal translation of Halo-halo is "Mix-mix". This iced dessert is a melange of sweet fruits, beans, tapioca, leche flan and ube jam, served with crushed ice, milk and sugar in a tall glass. Like a parfait, it yields a variety of flavors with every spoonful. Use as many or as few as you like of each ingredient listed.

3 ripe plantains (about 12 oz/350 g)
1/2 cup (200 g) sweetened red mung (*mongo*) beans, drained
1 cup (250 g) sweetened white beans, drained
1 1/2 cups (300 g) sweetened jackfruit, drained
1 cup (250 g) sweetened palm nuts (*kaong*), drained
1 cup (200 g) cooked sago pearls
1/2 cup (100 g) superfine sugar
Crushed ice
3 cups (750 ml) fresh milk
6 heaped tablespoons purple yam (*ube*) jam
Six 4-cm (1 1/2-in) slices Crème Caramel (see page 93), each slice quartered
1/2 cup (50 g) crispy rice cereal or toasted young rice (*pinipig*)
6 scoops ice-cream (any flavor)

1 Boil the plantains for 10 minutes or until tender. Peel and slice into 1-in (2 1/2-cm) pieces. Set aside to cool.

2 Divide the plantains, mung beans, white beans, jackfruit, palm nuts and sago equally between 6 tall dessert glasses and add sugar to taste.

3 Fill the glasses with crushed ice. Pour about 1/2 cup (125 ml) milk into each glass. Spoon the jam, Crème Caramel and crispy rice cereal or toasted rice on top of the crushed ice. Top each glass with a scoop of ice cream and serve with long-handled spoons.

The sweetened beans, jackfruits and palm nuts are sold in bottles in Asian grocery stores.

Serves 6
Preparation time: **20–30 mins**

Mixed Fruit Cocktail in Sweet Coconut Milk (Guinataan)

4 cups (1 liter) water
8 oz (225 g) sweet potatoes, peeled and cut into bite-sized pieces
5 oz (150 g) taro, peeled and cut into bite-sized pieces
8 oz (225 g) purple yam (*ube*), peeled and cut into bite-sized pieces
2–3 cups thickly sliced plantains
4 oz (120 g) rice flour
4 oz (120 g) sago pearls
$3^1/_2$ oz (100 g) fresh or canned jackfruit, cut into bite-sized pieces
$1^1/_2$ cups (375 ml) thick coconut milk
$1^1/_2$ cups (300 g) sugar

1 Bring the water to a boil in a stockpot. Add the sweet potatoes and taro and simmer over low heat for about 5 minutes. Add the yam and plantains and simmer for 4–5 minutes.
2 Moisten the rice flour with just enough water to make it sticky, then shape into small balls. Drop the rice flour balls, sago pearls and jackfruit into the liquid and continue to simmer. Stir in the thick coconut milk and sugar.
3 Simmer until all the ingredients are tender, about 20 minutes. When cooked, do not cover the pot or the dessert will spoil. Serve warm.

Sago pearls are tiny dried balls of sago obtained by grinding the pith of the sago palm to a paste and pressing it through a sieve. It is glutinous, with little taste and is often used in Asian desserts. Sago pearls should not be confused with fresh sago, which is starchy and sticky.

Serves 10–12
Preparation time: **40 mins**
Cooking time: **30 mins**

Milky Corn Surprise (Mais Con Hielo)

Part of the fun of eating this milky dessert lies in stabbing at the crushed ice to get to the bottom of the bowl, where the sweet corn lies. A truly refreshing dessert, this is a favorite of Filipinos.

Two 15-oz (415-g) cans cream-style corn
$^3/_4$ cup (150 g) sugar
3 cups (750 ml) evaporated milk or fresh cream
Crushed ice

1 Set aside six dessert bowls or tall dessert glasses. Spoon $^1/_2$ cup cream-style corn and 2 tablespoons sugar into each bowl or glass.

2 Pour $^1/_2$ cup milk or cream into each bowl then top with the crushed ice.

Serves 6
Preparation time: **5 mins**

Fresh Coconut Delight (Buko Salad)

This dessert combines young fresh coconut strips with canned fruits. A sweet, creamy concoction, Buko Salad is a favorite at Filipino gatherings.

2 cups (225 g) fresh young coconut strips
1 cup fresh or canned diced peaches, drained
$1/2$ cup fresh diced pineapple or one 15-oz (450-g) can tropical fruit cocktail, drained
1 cup (250 ml) whipping cream
1 cup (250 ml) sweetened condensed milk
8–10 maraschino cherries, to garnish (optional)

1 Toss the fresh coconut strips and diced fruits in a mixing bowl.
2 Add the whipping cream and condensed milk and mix well.
3 Chill for several hours in the refrigerator. Spoon into dessert bowls and top each portion with a cherry, if desired.

Young coconut strips, known in the Philippines as buko *strips, are sold in bottles in Asian grocery stores.*

Serves 8–10
Preparation time: **30 mins**
Chilling time: **3–4 hours**

Coconut Milk Pudding (Maja Blanca)

1¹/₂ cups (300 g) sugar
3 cups (750 ml) thin
coconut milk
2 cups (500 ml) fresh
cream or evaporated
milk
1 cup (200 g) cornstarch
Two 15 oz (450 g) cans
corn kernels, drained

Latik
1¹/₂ cups coconut cream

Serves 8
Preparation time: **40 mins**
Cooking time: **1 hour**

1 To make the Latik, stir the coconut cream over low heat. Simmer until the coconut oil separates from the solids and the coconut cream solids thicken and form thick, brown granules, about 30 minutes. Set aside the coconut oil and the Latik garnules.

2 Mix the sugar, thin coconut milk and cream or evaporated milk in a bowl. Set aside 1 cup of the mixture. Add the cornstarch to the reserved mixture and stir.

3 Heat the remaining mixture in a casserole over medium heat and bring to a boil. Add the corn and the cornstarch mixture. Stir until the mixture thickens. Add the reserved coconut oil a little at a time, if needed, to prevent the mixture from sticking to the casserole.

4 Pour into a buttered container and set aside to cool. When cool, remove the pudding from the container. Slice and sprinkle some Latik granules over each piece before serving.

Purple Yam Pudding (Haleyang Ube)

10–12 purple yams,
(about 4 lbs/2 kg)
1¹/₂ cups (375 ml)
evaporated milk
2¹/₃ cups (585 ml)
sweetened condensed
milk
1 cup (200 g) sugar
¹/₂ cup palm nuts
(*kaong*), optional

Serves 6–8
Preparation time: **30 mins**
Cooking time: **30 mins**

1 Boil the yams in water until tender. Peel then mash
the yams finely with a potato masher.
2 Put the mashed yam in a pot or wok. Pour in the
evaporated milk and condensed milk. Add the sugar.
Simmer gently over low heat, stirring continuously
with a wooden spoon to ensure the bottom does not
scorch.
3 Cook until the mixture thickens and becomes
difficult to stir.
4 Set aside to cool. Top with palm nuts, if desired,
then serve.

*Do not cover the yam pudding while it is still hot as
this will cause it to spoil.*

Crème Caramel (Leche Flan)

1 cup (150 g) dark
  brown sugar
¹/₄ cup (60 ml) water
6 eggs + 2 egg yolks
1¹/₂ cups (300 g) sugar
1¹/₂ cups (375 ml)
  cream or evaporated
  milk
2 tablespoons lime or
  lemon zest
4–5 thin slices lime, to
  garnish (optional)

Serves 4
Preparation time: **15 mins
  + 3–4 hours chilling time**
Cooking time: **1 hour**

1 Combine the sugar and water in a saucepan. Allow the sugar to melt over low heat until a syrup forms. Pour immediately into a loaf pan or casserole. Swirl the pan or dish to coat the bottom evenly. Set aside.
2 Lightly beat the eggs and egg yolks in a mixing bowl. Add sugar and cream or evaporated milk and stir. Strain the mixture then pour into the loaf pan or casserole. Stir in the lime or lemon zest.
3 Cover the pan or dish with aluminum foil. Place in a steamer and steam for about 1 hour or until the caramel is firm to the touch. Set aside to cool. Refrigerate for 3–4 hours or overnight before serving.
4 To serve, run a spatula or knife along the edge of the pan or dish to loosen the caramel. Turn out onto a serving platter and garnish with the lime slices if desired.

Rolled Meringue with Egg Yolk Filling
(Brazo de Mercedes)

Filling
8 egg yolks
1¼ cups (300 ml) condensed milk
2 tablespoons butter
1 tablespoon sugar
2 tablespoons lime or lemon zest

Meringue
8 egg whites
1 teaspoon cream of tartar
1¼ cups (250 g) sugar
1 teaspoon almond essence (optional)
½ cup (60 g) confectioners' sugar

Serves 8–10
Preparation time: **50 mins**
Cooking time: **10 mins**

1 To make the Filling, mix the egg yolks and condensed milk in a double boiler. Simmer, stirring constantly until the mixture starts to thicken, about 20 minutes. Add the butter and sugar and continue stirring for 5 more minutes.

2 Fold the lime or lemon zest into the mixture. Continue stirring over simmering water until the mixture turns light orange and thickens, 5–10 minutes. Remove from the heat and set aside.

3 To make the Meringue, beat the egg whites and cream of tartar in an electric mixer until soft peaks form. Gradually add the sugar and almond essence, if desired, and continue beating until stiff peaks form, about 10 minutes.

4 Preheat oven to 375°F (190°C). Line a greased baking tray with waxed paper and grease the waxed paper well. Sprinkle confectioners' sugar onto the waxed paper. Spread the egg white mixture on the paper, covering it entirely. Bake until the top is lightly browned, about 10 minutes.

5 Line a separate greased baking tray with waxed paper as before. Invert the Meringue onto this waxed paper so that the browned side faces down.

6 Spread the Filling on the Meringue. Fold in one side of the Meringue towards the middle. Fold the other side over to enclose the Filling. Dust with confectioners' sugar, cut into thin slices and serve.

Place the waxed paper on top of a greased baking tray and grease the paper.

Spread the egg white mixture on top of the confectioners' sugar.

Remove Meringue from tray. Place browned side down on a second greased baking tray.

Fold one side of meringue towards the middle, then the other to overlap.

Complete Recipe Listing